The Official
MANCHEST
An

CW00735041

Written by David Clayton, Designed by Simon Thorley

A Grange Publication

© 2011. Published by Grange Communications Ltd., Edinburgh, under licence from Manchester City Football Club. Printed in the EU.

Photographs © Press Association Images & Manchester City Football Club

ISBN 978-1-908221-29-2

£7.99

Contents

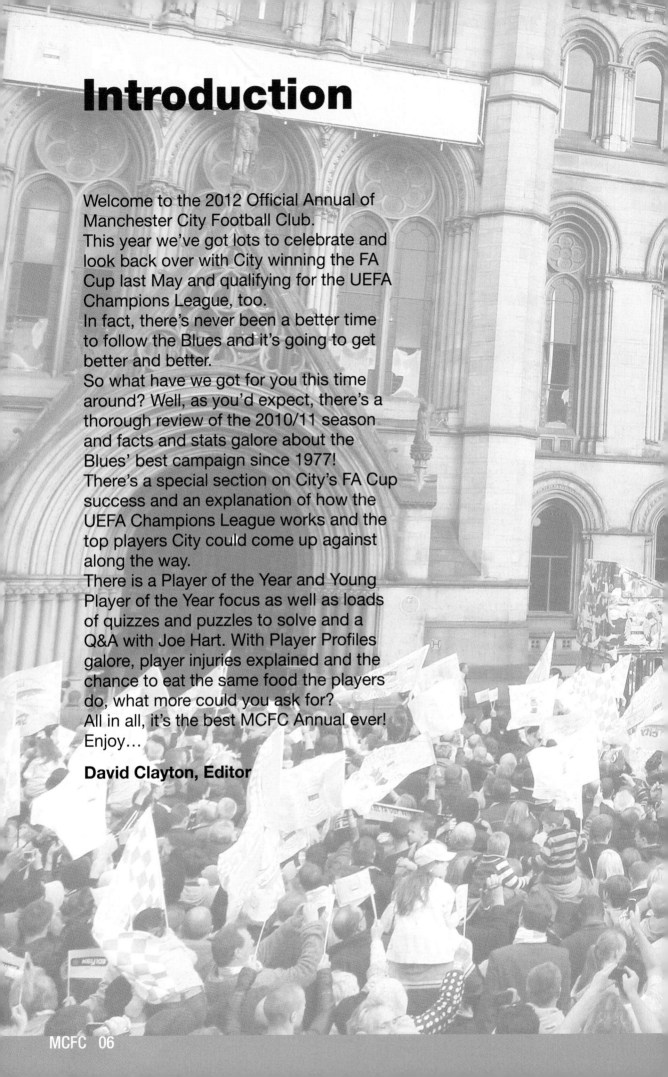

Introduction

Welcome to the 2012 Official Annual of Manchester City Football Club.
This year we've got lots to celebrate and look back over with City winning the FA Cup last May and qualifying for the UEFA Champions League, too.
In fact, there's never been a better time to follow the Blues and it's going to get better and better.
So what have we got for you this time around? Well, as you'd expect, there's a thorough review of the 2010/11 season and facts and stats galore about the Blues' best campaign since 1977!
There's a special section on City's FA Cup success and an explanation of how the UEFA Champions League works and the top players City could come up against along the way.
There is a Player of the Year and Young Player of the Year focus as well as loads of quizzes and puzzles to solve and a Q&A with Joe Hart. With Player Profiles galore, player injuries explained and the chance to eat the same food the players do, what more could you ask for?
All in all, it's the best MCFC Annual ever! Enjoy…

David Clayton, Editor

MCFC 07

Mancini's Message

Welcome to The Official Manchester City Annual 2012!

Last season was a very special one for the Club and it was the first trophy we have won for 35 years, which means most of the people reading this weren't even born when we last won a cup!

As the manager, I was very proud to lead the team out at Wembley and also into the UEFA Champions League for the first time, but it was down to the players who worked very hard all season.

During the 2011/12 season, we hope to do even better! Our aim is to keep improving until we reach our goal so we will continue to work hard and concentrate.

The Official Manchester City Annual 2012 will, I have no doubt, keep you entertained for many hours with a great selection of features on the players.

So enjoy this and thank you for your fantastic support!

Roberto Mancini

2010/11 Season
Premier League Review

City achieved their highest ever Premier League finish last season – this is the story of how history was made...

AUGUST
PLD: 3 W: 1 D: 1 L: 1 F: 3 A: 1

It all began at White Hart Lane with a game against one of the teams many people believed could be a surprise challenger for the Premier League title – Tottenham. City's record against Spurs in recent years isn't good and the Blues had to rely on a Joe Hart wonder show to leave with a precious 0-0 draw. Had he not been at his brilliant best, Roberto Mancini's side could easily have left with a heavy defeat and the whole season ahead would have taken on a different look.

As it was, confidence was high going into the first home game of the campaign and City brushed aside Liverpool with ease, winning 3-0 with goals from Gareth Barry and Carlos Tevez (2) putting the Blues fourth in the table.

Next up were Sunderland at the Stadium of Light and City were by far the better team for the first hour or so, but a miss by Tevez in the first-half made the travelling fans wonder if it might be 'one of those days' – it was. Deep into injury time, Micah Richards was adjudged to have pushed Darren Bent as he went for a header and the ref gave a penalty – which Bent scored to give Sunderland a 1-0 win.

SEPTEMBER
PLD: 3 W: 2 D: 1 L: 0 F: 4 A: 1

Things didn't improve much for the next game, either. Blackburn Rovers were expected to be beaten easily at the City of Manchester Stadium, but a mix-up between Hart and Kolo Toure allowed Rovers to take a shock lead and only a Patrick Vieira goal saved City's blushes by earning a 1-1 draw. Mancini's side then made the short journey up the motorway to play Wigan Athletic and almost 5,000 City fans left happy having seen a terrific goal by Tevez and Yaya Toure's first for the club give the

Blues a well-deserved 2-0 win.
There was better to come, too, following a disappointing Carling Cup exit at West Brom in midweek, City bounced back in style to beat Chelsea 1-0 courtesy of a Tevez special – a win that proved the Blues were more than a match for the best.

2010/11 Season
Premier League Review

OCTOBER
PLD: 4 W: 2 D: 0 L: 2 F: 6 A: 8

October proved to be one of the shakiest months in City's season, though it started well enough with a hard-fought 2-1 home win over Newcastle United. Though Tevez had put the Blues ahead on 18 minutes from the spot, the Geordies battled well and levelled before Adam Johnson climbed off the subs' bench to fire home a late winner.

Another side tipped for relegation, Blackpool, also gave Mancini's side a tough afternoon with City unable to dominate in the way most had expected. In a see-saw game, two goals from Tevez and a late third from David Silva – his first for the club – proved just enough to beat Ian Holloway's entertainers 3-2 – a win that put City second in the table.

A week later, the Blues came back to earth with a crash. Despite dominating the opening minutes against Arsenal, a mistimed tackle by Dedryck Boyata saw the young defender shown a red card and City face almost 80 minutes with just ten men. Eventually, the visitors made the extra man count and ran out convincing 3-0 winners.

Then the Blues lost again, throwing a 1-0 lead at Wolves away to lose 2-1. Silva won a penalty midway through the first half and Emmanuel Adebayor tucked home the spot-kick, but Wolves came back strongly to level before the break and win the game with another in the second half.

NOVEMBER
PLD: 5 W: 2 D: 3 L: 0 F: 7 A: 2

November proved to be a mixed month in many ways. It started well with a clinical 2-0 win at West Brom thanks to two Mario Balotelli goals, but the fiery Italian was then sent off leaving his team-mates to battle most of the second half without him.

Then followed a disappointing midweek home derby against Manchester United – one of the most boring for years – with neither team looking as though they were willing to risk losing by going for the win and the 0-0 draw was no more than either side deserved.

At least Birmingham at home a few days later offered City the chance to get back to winning ways, but the visitors put up a dogged display and left with a well-earned 0-0 draw – a result that had the City fans booing their side off.

Things had to improve away to Fulham – and did they ever! With City taking on former manager Mark Hughes, the Blues turned on a blistering performance to go in 3-0 up at half-time thanks to goals from Tevez, Pablo Zabaleta and Yaya Toure. Another Tevez goal just after half-time sealed the points and a 4-1 win for a team many believed couldn't play fast, attacking football.

It looked like City would follow that win with another away from home at Stoke, particularly when Richards scored a great solo goal on 81 minutes to give the Blues a 1-0 lead. Unfortunately, the Potters scored a late equaliser to spoil the party and deny the visitors victory.

2010/11 Season
Premier League Review

DECEMBER
PLD: 5 W: 4 D: 1 L: 0 F: 12 A: 4

City clicked into gear in December with 12 points out of a possible 15 moving Mancini's side into second in the Premier League by the start of the New Year.

The month began well with Tevez's third-minute goal enough to beat Bolton 1-0 at the City of Manchester Stadium and the Blues followed that up with a comfortable 3-1 win at West Ham, where Yaya Toure, a Robert Green own goal and Adam Johnson scored the goals.

Jinx team Everton again proved to be unlucky as they inflicted yet another win over the Blues at the City of Manchester Stadium, winning 2-1 and even scoring the Blues' only goal thanks to a Phil Jagielka own goal on 72 minutes.

However, Mancini's men bounced back in style to beat Newcastle 3-1 at St James' Park on Boxing Day. City raced out of the blocks and were 2-0 up with just five minutes gone thanks to a Tevez goal on two minutes and a Gareth Barry effort on five. Tevez added a late third to seal the points and put City up to second place behind Manchester United.

Two days later the Blues went one better, beating Aston Villa 4-0 at the City of Manchester Stadium with Mario Balotelli scoring a hat-trick and Joleon Lescott adding another in an impressive display.

every day

JANUARY
PLD: 4 W: 2 D: 1 L: 1 F: 5 A: 4

City went into the New Year brimming with confidence but had to rely on Adam Johnson's solitary goal to see off Blackpool 1-0. It was the second time the Seasiders had pushed the Blues all the way and left with nothing to show for their efforts. A midweek trip to Arsenal then yielded another important point with the Blues putting up a dogged defensive display to earn a valuable 0-0 draw at the Emirates Stadium.

Four goals in 26 minutes seemed to have killed off Wolves in the Blues' next home game, with Kolo Toure, Tevez (2) and Yaya Toure giving City a 4-1 lead over Mick McCarthy's side, but Wolves never gave up and two late goals meant the hosts were clinging on to a 4-3 lead right until the final whistle. That win briefly put the Blues top of the Premier league table, too.

Then Darren Bent came back to haunt City! The former Sunderland striker became Aston Villa's record signing during the January transfer window – City had signed Edin Dzeko from Wolfsburg, too – and it was Bent's first-half goal that proved enough to give Villa a precious 1-0 win at Villa Park, despite City dominating the second half and hitting the post twice.

FEBRUARY
PLD: 4 W: 1 D: 2 L: 1 F: 7 A: 5

With the title race hotting up and City still in touching distance of leaders United, there could be no slip-ups during February – but there proved to be several.

Goals from Tevez and Kolarov twice gave City the lead at Birmingham, but the Midlanders came back to level each time and earn a 2-2 draw.

A first-half Tevez hat-trick was enough to see off West Brom at the City of Manchester Stadium and send the Blues into the Old Trafford Manchester derby in great spirit. In fact, City would dominate much of the first-half before a lapse in concentration allowed Nani to race through and give United the lead just before half-time.

When Dzeko's shot hit Silva to level scores on 65 minutes, it seemed like Mancini's men would go on and win the game, but a spectacular late winner from Wayne Rooney undid all the previous hard work and gave United a 2-1 win they hardly deserved.

With the Blues progressing well in the Europa League and FA Cup, the next home game against Fulham was something of a wet lettuce, with Balotelli's first-half goal wiped out by Damien Duff after the break. It was a disappointing draw because it saw the Blues lose further ground in the title race and with Spurs breathing down their necks, every point dropped threatened the hopes of a UEFA Champions League spot.

MARCH
PLD: 2 W: 1 D: 0 L: 1 F: 1 A: 2

Though City played six games in March, only two of them were in the Premier League and the first of those matches was against Wigan at home. Silva's fortuitous goal on 38 minutes proved enough to beat the relegation-threatened visitors and keep City third but it would be 15 days before the next Premier League game.

After last season's 4-2 win at Chelsea, hopes were high that the Blues could leave Stamford Bridge with another victory, but the loss of Tevez before kick-off was a major blow and City never really looked like scoring during a disappointing 2-0 defeat – a loss that ended any lingering hopes of winning the title.

2010/11 Season
Premier League Review

APRIL
PLD: 3 W: 2 D: 0 L: 1 F: 6 A: 3

City powered into April by thrashing Sunderland 5-0 at the City of Manchester Stadium thanks to goals from Johnson, Tevez, Silva, Vieira and Yaya Toure. It was just the tonic Mancini's men needed as they entered the final stretch of the season, but the next game would see the biggest win of the campaign followed by the biggest loss.

An out-of-sorts City were brushed aside by Liverpool at Anfield and were 3-0 down by half-time, with Luis Suarez and Andy Carroll causing the City defence problems all evening. Losing skipper Tevez early on with a hamstring injury only made matters worse on a night to forget for the Blues.

By the time City travelled to Ewood Park to face Blackburn Rovers, Tottenham were just a few points behind and gathering momentum, but with the game seemingly heading for a 0-0 draw and Blackburn looking the likelier side to snatch a later winner, Edin Dzeko climbed off the bench to score a dramatic 75th-minute goal that gave the Blues vital breathing space in the battle to finish in the top four.

MAY
PLD: 5 W: 4 D: 0 L: 1 F: 9 A: 3

City saved their best month of the season for last, with a brilliant 12 points from their last five games. It had been an exhausting season, but Mancini's men could see the finishing line and one last big effort would see them home. It began with a narrow 2-1 win over West Ham – this despite goals from Nigel de Jong (at last!) and Zabaleta putting City 2-0 up after just 15 minutes.

The only blip in May would come away to – who else? – Everton, where despite playing some wonderful football and going in at half-time 1-0 up through Yaya Toure's 28th-minute goal, the Toffees rallied to score twice in five minutes after the break and beat City – yet again – 2-1.

Spurs failed to close the gap by dropping points against Blackpool, so City knew a win over Harry Redknapp's team a few days later would all but guarantee UEFA Champions League football for the Blues. In a tense, exciting game, James Milner's low cross was turned in by Peter Crouch – the same player who had ended City's hopes of a top four finish the season before – to give the Blues a vital 1-0 win. There was now no way Spurs or Liverpool could catch City and it confirmed a top four finish for the Blues.

Then third-placed Arsenal lost at home to Aston Villa and suddenly maximum points from the final two games would mean City finishing third and not having to play a qualifying game to go into the UEFA Champions League group stages.

With the FA Cup now won, City took on Stoke in a re-arranged game and two Tevez crackers and a Lescott header gave the Blues a 3-0 win and also a leap-frog over Arsenal.

With just one game left, as long as City matched Arsenal's result or bettered it, third place was guaranteed. Bolton away was never going to be an easy game but a bizarre Lescott goal just before half-time and another from Dzeko meant the Blues got their reward for a magnificent end to a fantastic season.

Player of the Year
Vincent Kompany

City's hugely popular defender Vincent Kompany enjoyed an outstanding season and was a worthy recipient of the main prize at the MCFC Awards 2011.

His commanding displays at centre-half helped his team to 30 cleans sheets last season and just like the team, Kompany got stronger and stronger as the campaign progressed. After joining the club from Hamburg in 2008, Kompany moved effortlessly from midfield to defence and produced many match-winning performances. He led the Blues out at Wembley for the FA Cup semi-final against Manchester United, with his last-ditch blocks and tackles inspiring City to a 1-0 win and, eventually, the FA Cup Final itself where he was equally commanding against Stoke City.

On collecting his award, the ever-modest Belgian was quick to heap praise on his team-mates: "It's an unbelievable sign of recognition and I'm so happy about it," he said. "But for me, this is not about individual awards. It's about recognising the team and without the team none of this would have happened. I'm delighted but I know who I owe it to. "You expect your fellow players to know the most about it, they see you every day so it was great to get this, but it could have been any of us which is a sign of how strong we've been as a team. I thank my team-mates, but the thing that stood out for me was us winning the FA Cup."

The ever-modest Belgian was the Blues' outstanding player on so many occasions last season that his consistently high levels became accepted as the norm and whether he was partnered by Kolo Toure or Joleon Lescott, Kompany was never less than a rock in the back four – but he won't stop with one good season. Kompany's aim is to be the best he can be and if he continues to improve at the rate he is at present that means being the best defender in the world.

Focused, determined and dependable – Vincent Kompany has the lot. Thank goodness he's a City player!

Midfield magician David Silva came in second with skipper Carlos Tevez third in a contest that could also easily have seen Joe Hart, Nigel de Jong, Pablo Zabaleta or Micah Richards win as well.

The Story of the 2011 FA Cup

City ended their long wait to win a trophy by lifting the FA Cup last May – but how did it happen…?

They say winning the FA Cup is part luck, part desire and City had a bit of both along the way to a first FA Cup Final in 30 years. There were thrills, spills and for once, no heartaches on a breathless journey to the final tie against Stoke City in May.
Here's the Road to Wembley with all the details you need to know…

Third Round:
LEICESTER CITY 2 CITY 2
A full-house at The Walker's Stadium and a game against former manager Sven-Goran Eriksson – all the ingredients needed for an exciting FA Cup tie – and that's exactly what we got! Leicester were ahead inside the first minute through a Sol Bamba header, but goals from James Milner and Carlos Tevez put City 2-1 up at the break. The Foxes didn't deserve to lose so when Paul Gallagher levelled following a mistake by Joe Hart, it gave them the draw their spirited display deserved.
Att: 31,200

Third Round (replay):
CITY 4 LEICESTER 2
City were in no mood to fluff their lines knowing Notts County awaited the winners in the next round and goals from Tevez, Patrick Vieira and Adam Johnson put the Blues 3-1 up at the break. Leicester never gave up, pulled another goal back and it took Aleksandar Kolarov's 90th-minute goal to ensure the visitors didn't pinch a late equaliser and seal a 4-2 win.
Att: 27,755

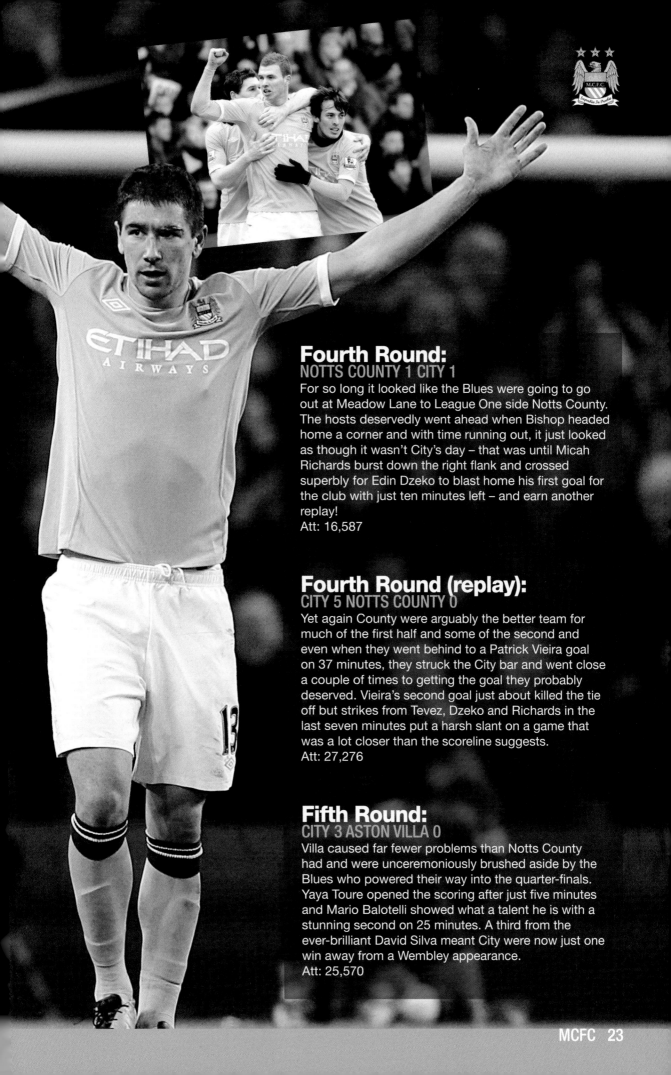

Fourth Round:
NOTTS COUNTY 1 CITY 1

For so long it looked like the Blues were going to go out at Meadow Lane to League One side Notts County. The hosts deservedly went ahead when Bishop headed home a corner and with time running out, it just looked as though it wasn't City's day – that was until Micah Richards burst down the right flank and crossed superbly for Edin Dzeko to blast home his first goal for the club with just ten minutes left – and earn another replay!

Att: 16,587

Fourth Round (replay):
CITY 5 NOTTS COUNTY 0

Yet again County were arguably the better team for much of the first half and some of the second and even when they went behind to a Patrick Vieira goal on 37 minutes, they struck the City bar and went close a couple of times to getting the goal they probably deserved. Vieira's second goal just about killed the tie off but strikes from Tevez, Dzeko and Richards in the last seven minutes put a harsh slant on a game that was a lot closer than the scoreline suggests.

Att: 27,276

Fifth Round:
CITY 3 ASTON VILLA 0

Villa caused far fewer problems than Notts County had and were unceremoniously brushed aside by the Blues who powered their way into the quarter-finals. Yaya Toure opened the scoring after just five minutes and Mario Balotelli showed what a talent he is with a stunning second on 25 minutes. A third from the ever-brilliant David Silva meant City were now just one win away from a Wembley appearance.

Att: 25,570

Sixth Round:
CITY 1 READING 0

Reading had already done City a massive favour by beating jinx team Everton in the previous round but their reward was to exit the last eight thanks to a Micah Richards header on 74 minutes. Up until then, the Royals had looked good for a replay and had impressed the home fans with their organisation and effort. Richards soared to head home a corner and send the Blues to a Wembley semi-final and mean Mancini's side were just 90 minutes away from the Final itself....
Att: 41,150

Semi-Final:
CITY 1 MANCHESTER UNITED 0

An unforgettable day for the 35,000 City fans who made their way to Wembley for the highest-profile Manchester derby of all-time. City had lost Tevez through injury and United were without Wayne Rooney who was suspended, but it was the Reds who began the better side and but for two incredible Joe Hart saves, they would have gone ahead. The Blues clung on and began to finally believe in themselves, ending the half the better team. Then, just seven minutes after the break, the Blue half of Wembley erupted! A poor pass by Michael Carrick was intercepted by Yaya Toure who powered forward and past Nemanja Vidic before rolling the ball through Edwin van der Sar's legs for the only goal of the game. City deserved to win and despite a nervy last few minutes, the win never looked in any doubt.
Att: 86,549

FA Cup Final:
CITY 1 STOKE CITY 0

With Stoke easily beating Bolton in the other semi-final, the Potters fans wondered whether it was their time to win the FA Cup – this was the first FA Cup Final in Stoke's history! But they were facing a City team who believed the trophy's destiny was heading in their direction and they played in a way that suggested they never thought they would lose. The Blues dominated the game but a mix of poor finishing and great goalkeeping by Thomas Sorensen meant that when a long ball found Kenwyne Jones with time running out, all he had to do was beat Joe Hart as he raced towards goal – Hart saved and the chance was gone. Then, with City building up a head of steam, Silva's cross caused panic, a clearance was blocked by Mario Balotelli and the ball fell to Yaya Toure to lash home and send the City fans wild. It proved to be the winner too, and gave City their first trophy for 35 years – what a day!
Att: 85,000

Wordsearch

Can you find the names of 10 City players in the wordsearch puzzle below? Remember, the words can go upwards, downwards, sideways and diagonally - good luck!

Balotelli Boyata De Jong Dzeko Johnson Kompany
Lescott Richards Silva Zabaleta

```
D W F Y M G I J Z L Y
K B K P N J L O M N N
K C M O B O L H T B A
C S J A K J E N J B P
H E I E T B T S D R M
D F Z L O E O O T T O
M D K Y V M L N L K K
D R A N W A A A L V X
M T N G N N B M B T H
A S D R A H C I R A L
L E S C O T T T K P C Z
```

Singing the Blues

Here's a selection of City songs you'll hear down at the City of Manchester Stadium on a matchday…

Blue Moon
'Blue Moon,
You saw me standing alone,
Without a dream in my heart,
Without a love of my own.'

We're not really here
'We are not; we're not really here,
We are not; we're not really here,
Like the fans of the Invisible Man,
We're not really here.'

You are my City
'You are my City, my only City,
You make me happy,
When skies are grey,
You'll never know just,
How much I love you,
So please don't take my City away.'

Best team in the world…
'City! City!
The best team in the land,
In all the world.'

Yaya Toure to the tune of 'Hey Jude' by The Beatles
'Ya, Ya, Ya,
Ya, Ya, Ya, Ya,
Ya, Ya, YaYa Toure

When De Jong goes sliding in
'Oh when De Jong,
Goes sliding in, Oh when De Jong
goes sliding in,
There's only going to be one winner,
Oh when De Jong goes sliding in!'

Let's all do the Poznan
'Let's all do the Poznan,
Let's all do the Poznan
Na, na, na, na!
Na, na, na, na!'

Guess Who?

See if you can work out which City player is disguised...

Answer on page 60

Spot The Difference

Study Picture A closely and then look at Picture B – Picture B has SIX differences – can you spot them all? Circle each one you find and see if you can find them all...

Answers on page 60

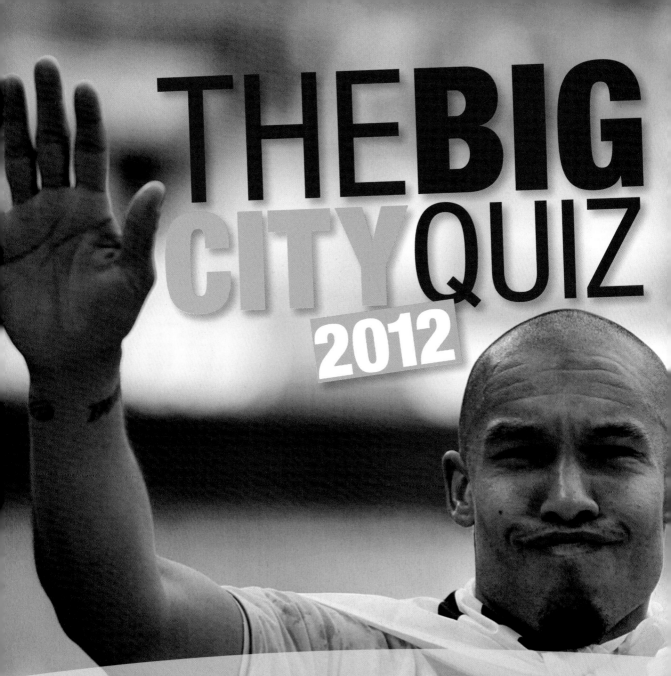

THE BIG CITY QUIZ 2012

1. WHAT IS MARIO BALOTELLI'S DOG CALLED?

2. NAME THE TEAM ROBERTO MANCINI MANAGED BEFORE HE CAME TO CITY.

3. WHO SCORED CITY'S VITAL EQUALISING GOAL AT NOTTS COUNTY IN THE FA CUP?

4. WHAT NATIONALITY IS ALEKSANDAR KOLAROV?

5. HOW MANY CLEAN SHEETS DID JOE HART KEEP IN TOTAL LAST SEASON? A) 25 B) 27 C) 29

6. WHO WAS THE ONLY TEAM TO BEAT CITY HOME AND AWAY DURING THE 2010/11 SEASON?

7. WHO SCORED CITY'S WINNING GOAL IN THE HOME GAME AGAINST TOTTENHAM LAST SEASON?

8. HOW MANY GOALS DID MARIO BALOTELLI SCORE AGAINST ASTON VILLA LAST SEASON?

9. WHO KNOCKED CITY OUT OF THE EUROPA LEAGUE IN 2011?

10. DARREN BENT SCORED A WINNING GOAL FOR TWO DIFFERENT CLUBS AGAINST CITY LAST SEASON. TRUE OR FALSE?

Think you know everything you need to know about City? Well, test your knowledge to the full in our Big City Quiz...

11. HOW MANY GOALS DID CITY SCORE IN LAST SEASON'S FA CUP RUN? A) 18 B) 19 C)20

12. WHO SCORED HIS FIRST EVER CITY GOAL AGAINST WEST HAM IN APRIL 2011?

13. WHICH TOP AWARD DID MARIO BALOTELLI WIN IN 2010? A) ITALIAN PLAYER OF THE YEAR B) THE GOLDEN BOY AWARD C) GOLDEN BOOT

14. CITY'S PITCH WAS VOTED BEST IN THE PREMIER LEAGUE FOR 2010/11. TRUE OR FALSE?

15. JOE HART STARTED AND ENDED LAST SEASON BY KEEPING HOW MANY CLEAN SHEETS IN A ROW? A) 2 B) 3 C) 4

16. WHICH CLUB DID EDIN DZEKO JOIN CITY FROM?

17. YAYA TOURE PLAYED FOR BARCELONA IN THE 2009

UEFA CHAMPIONS LEAGUE FINAL. TRUE OR FALSE?

18. WHICH SPANISH ISLAND WAS DAVID SILVA BORN ON?

19. WHICH SQUAD NUMBER DID CITY RETIRE WHEN MARC VIVIEN FOE DIED?

20. WHICH BAND PLAYED SELL-OUT CONCERTS AT THE CITY OF MANCHESTER STADIUM AFTER THE 2010/11 SEASON ENDED?

Answers on page 61

We Can Be Heroes

Just for one day...

Guess Who?

See if you can work out who the four City players disguised below are...

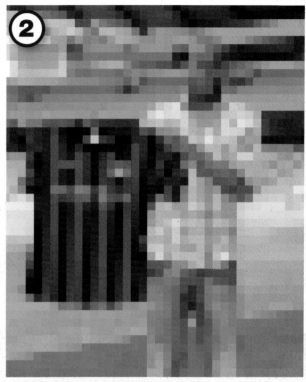

manc

Crossword

Fill the puzzle by answering the clues below

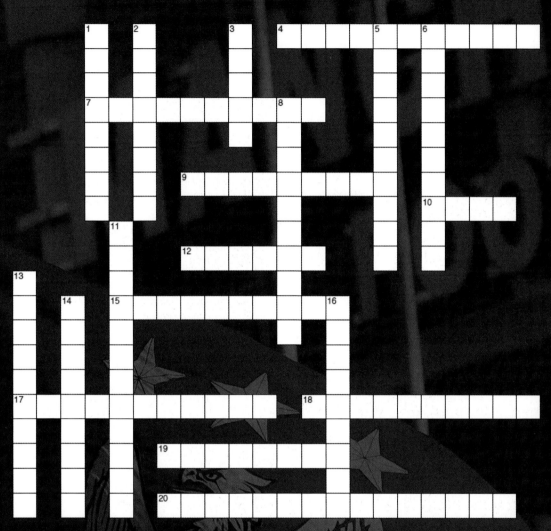

ACROSS

4 Current City player who played for Leeds, Newcastle and Aston Villa (5, 6)

7 Team that knocked City out of the 2010/11 Europa League (6, 4)

9 Yaya Toure's last club (9)

10 FC Salzburg player City fans 'adopted' last season (4)

12 Country Edin Dzeko was born in (6)

15 Former England player who is on Roberto Mancini's coaching staff (5, 5)

17 City's Dutch midfield ace (5, 2, 4)

18 Award Carlos Tevez shared for scoring 20 Premier League goals (6, 4)

19 City fans' favourite song (4, 4)

20 City will play in this for the first time in 2011/12 (9, 6)

DOWN

1 Country City's owners come from (3, 5)

2 City's female mascot (8)

3 The name of Mario Balotelli's dog (5)

5 Balotelli's nickname (5, 5)

6 Country both Yaya and Kolo Toure play for (5, 5)

8 Team Roberto Mancini managed before City (5, 5)

11 Award Joe Hart won for keeping 17 Premier League clean sheets (6, 6)

13 Where City's training ground is based (10)

14 Goalkeeper who was Joe Hart's No.2 in Season 2010/11 (4, 5)

16 A dance you might see at a City home game - or away game! (3, 6)

Answers on page 61

Young Player of the Year
Mario Balotelli

'Super' Mario Balotelli ended his first season as a City player by picking up the Young Player of the Year award as voted for by the official MCFC Supporters' Club, completing a highly satisfying first year in England following a high-profile move from Inter Milan in 2010.

The young Italian has a knack of attracting bizarre headlines in the newspapers, but the City fans quickly took him to their hearts after a very impressive first season in sky blue. Now, the Golden Boy of European football (an award he picked up in December 2010 for being voted the brightest talent in Europe), has the world at his feet and it is up to him to decide how big a star he becomes.

Mario netted his first City goal after coming on as a substitute against FC Timisoara in the Europa League, but suffered a setback when he sustained a knee injury in the same game that kept him sidelined until October.

After making a full recovery, he scored two goals against West Bromwich Albion, opening his Barclays Premier League account in style before being sent off - if ever a game summed up his talent and ability to frustrate, that was it!

One thing is for sure, there is never a dull moment when Mario is around! Away from football he loves animals and visited Knowsley Safari Park and the Manchester Dogs Home during his spare time and even has a pet rescued dog named Lucky back in Italy.

A Premier League hat-trick against Aston Villa during a 4-0 victory demonstrated that Balotelli was more than capable of producing the goods and he became a regular in Roberto Mancini's team and a sublime strike against the same team in the FA Cup later in the year proved what an explosive talent he can be.

The youngster produced a man-of-the-match display during City's FA Cup final against Stoke at Wembley, helping the Blues to a 1-0 victory and he also earned praise for his performance against Manchester United in the 1-0 win during the semi-final.

With 10 goals from just 18 starts, Mario's first campaign has been impressive and full of promise and his season ended with a recall from Cesare Prandelli to the Italy squad for the Euro 2012 qualifier against Estonia in Modena.

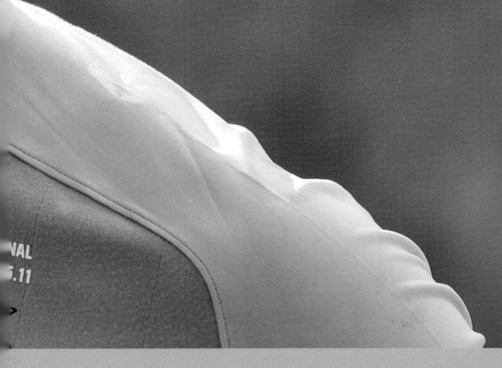

UEFA Champions League Qualification and Group Stages

City's historic third-place Premier League finish meant automatic entry into the Group Stages of European football's elite competition for the first time.

The Blues had only once before entered the premier tournament of champions when it was under its former guise of the European Cup when Joe Mercer's side played Turkish side Fenerbahce, drawing 0-0 at Maine Road and exiting after a 2-1 defeat in the second leg.

The competition began on June 28 with a First Qualifying Round made up from four clubs and the two winners progressed to the Second Qualifying Round which began on July 12 and saw the entrance of 32 champions from UEFA-ranked countries that were positioned 17 to 42 in the 2012 qualification list.

Among the teams who entered at this stage were Shamrock Rovers, Maccabi Haifa, Rosenberg, Malmo, Linfield and Bangor City and 17 teams then progressed to the Third Qualifying Round which was a mix of champions from higher ranked countries, runners-up and the clubs who progressed from the previous round.

The 17 winners from the above then went into the Third Round which saw the entry of 13 even stronger sides including Benfica, Rangers, FC Copenhagen and two sides the Blues faced in the 2010/11 Europa League in FC Timisoara and Dynamo Kyiv. This began on July 26.

Phew! It's a big competition!!

Just 15 teams made the Play-off Round – the round the Blues would have entered into had we not overtaken Arsenal in the final stretch of last season - and the quality of the sides involved illustrate the reason Roberto Mancini was so keen to avoid finishing fourth!

Arsenal were joined by Bayern Munich, Udinese, Villarreal and a third-place finishing French side plus the 15 winners from the Third Round for the right to play in the Group Stages and this began on August 16.

Finally, after the second legs were completed on August 24, the draw for the groups took place in Monaco a day later. This is where the 22 elite sides entered and joined the 10 teams who had qualified for the right to join them.

Eight groups of four will then battle out the Group Stages, with the top two teams going into the last 16 – the knockout stage – plus eight more best-finishing third placed teams going into the Europa League Round of 32.

The Group Stages began on September 13 and 14 – the first steps towards the UEFA Champions League Final in Munich on 19 May 2012 – keep your diary free!

Up on the Catwalk

Gareth Barry: *Pauses before making his way back down the catwalk*

Former goalkeeper Shay Given and Vincent Kompany: *In front of an army of photographers and phone-cams*

FA Cup Strut: *The boys do one last parade with their recently-acquired trophy*

Edin Dzeko: *Strikes a pose*

The Story of the Poznan

Here we look at the history behind the Blues' now infamous backwards pogo...the Poznan

SO how exactly did 'The Poznan' begin? Well, it's the dance craze City fans adopted earlier in the 2010/11 season and something that has grabbed headlines throughout the football world, mainly because it's fun, good natured and looks fantastic.

But where and when did City fans 'adopt' the dance? To find the answer to this we need to go back to the home leg of the Europa League group stages when the Blues played Polish side Lech Poznan at the City of Manchester Stadium.

Just over 2,000 visiting Poles were in loud voice before and during the game until something nobody – apart from the visitors – had ever seen before began to happen. The Lech fans turned their backs in unison, linked arms or put them around the shoulders of whoever was next to them, and began to jump up and down. It looked bizarre but fantastic at the same time.

So the seeds of 'The Poznan' were born.

There were attempts at the next few home games but against Bolton in early December, it finally seemed to click until by early New Year, City fans were doing The Poznan as if it had always been ours.

Gradually, more and more City fans began to do it,

usually to the chant of "Let's all do the Poznan, let's all do the Poznan!" until, by February, there were games when the whole stadium was doing it – and it looked incredible.

The best was still to come, however....

When 35,000 City fans crammed into one half of Wembley began to do the Poznan before the semi-final against Manchester United. The feat was repeated when the United team was read out and, of course, just after Yaya Toure scored the winning goal. The world sat up and took notice with the Poznan featured on news stories around the world and as the players celebrated both the semi-final and FA Cup Final victories, they, in turn, did their own Poznan to the delight of the City fans.

Others have tried to copy it but the fact is, it now belongs to the City fans more than even those who first introduced it to us.

And remember, if any other team tries to do it, just sing "Shall we show you what to do?" then turn around as one and start to jump. That's how you do the Poznan!

Wordsearch

Find the 10 City-related words or names hidden in the grid. Words can go horizontally, vertically and diagonally in all eight directions.

BLUE MOON CARRINGTON CITY SQUARE DAVID PLATT ETIHAD
MANCINI MOONBEAM MOONCHESTER POZNAN SKY BLUE

```
N W R E T S E H C N O O M
B T X L G Y C Y G B N X Z
T K F C A R R I N G T O N
B L J D H J C I L T C D L
C N T R W T N Z M T I K W
S Z A V P I G O N A T H B
H K T N C T O N O L Y G D
R M Y N Z N F D O P S W M
F M A B B O A G M D Q R C
Z M C E L H P T E I U G D
M T A L I U J R U V A R F
T M F T M N E L L A R R R
Z T E R T C G T B D E W P
```

Answers on page 61

Spot The Difference

Time for some more detective work! Study Picture A closely and then look at Picture B – Picture B has SIX differences – can you spot them all? Circle each one you find and see if you can find them all...

Answers on page 60

Eat Like A Player

Here's your chance to cook up and eat what a professional footballer has to keep him fit...

Baked Salmon with warm Nicoise salad

Method:
- Place the salmon on a roasting tray and season it. Bake for 10-15 mins at gas mark 6
- Combine diced new potatoes, black olives, sunblushed tomatoes, green beans with dressing, and warm gently (microwave for one minute is fine)
- Lay a salad base, placing the cooked fish on top

Why we cook this dish:
- Low fat – needs no explanation!
- High protein – vital for healthy diet
- Carbohydrates – for slow-releasing energy

Ingredients:
(serves four)
4 x 6oz fillets of skinless salmon
100g cooked new potatoes
75g black olives
Sunblushed or cherry tomatoes
Green beans

Dressing:
Zest of one lemon
Teaspoon of grain mustard
1/4 cup extra-virgin olive oil
Salt
Pepper

Favourite meal of:
WAYNE BRIDGE

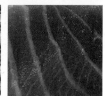

Eat Like A Player

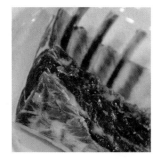

Crusted rack of lamb with new potatoes

Method:
- Seal off your racks of lamb on all sides in a hot pan, whilst warming the honey in a separate pan
- When sealed, dip the fat side of the lamb into the honey before covering with crushed pistachios
- Place the now crusted lamb into the oven for 14 minutes at 180 degrees (gas mark 6) for a medium rare finish, but longer depending on how you like it
- Boil the new potatoes for 20 minutes before crushing them, add a sautéed onion and finely chopped chives to the mix, before putting into a 2inch ring to make the cake
- Cut the carrots into batons and steam for 6 minutes
- Cut the meat down the middle and plate up as it is in the picture

Why we cook this dish:
The rack of lamb is a lean cut of meat, so it is a healthy option. The potatoes provide carbohydrates for the players' energy, and the other vegetables are obviously very good for you, too

Ingredients:
(serves four)
4 racks of lamb
200ml honey
200g pistachios
800g new potatoes
Small bunch of chives
1 onion
2 large carrots
300g curly kale

Favourite meal of:
JOE HART

Inside the Injury

Club doctor Jamie Butler explains how players' injuries are diagnosed and treated..

NO:1 Dislocation

INVESTIGATION:

When a joint is ruptured, the bones separate, the capsule breaks and the two bones that form the joint come apart. With a ball and socket joint, it is when the humerus (ball) comes away from the adrenal part of the scapula (socket). The shoulder is an unstable joint due to the amount of movement that you get from it. If you have dislocated your shoulder once, you are more likely to do so again. Goalkeepers are most vulnerable to this as when they are diving, their arm goes behind their head, and the armpit hits the ground which gives them less protection.

DIAGNOSIS:

If it is a first time dislocation there will be a lot of pain and they'll know about it. They may even have heard a pop. They feel a crack; they may have broken the bone in the arm as well as the dislocation. Sometimes they will feel numbness in what we call a 'badge' area, which is where the auxiliary nerve is and they could have symptoms of pins and needles going down to the hand. There may be neck pain, sometimes some tingling, and they won't want to move their arm. You would be able to diagnose it on the pitch. Invariably they will have their shirt off and you will administer pain relief, which is the gas and air which we carry as a medical team. Sometimes the

shoulder will just pop back in, which can be a painful procedure in itself.

TREATMENT:

This can vary. You have the non-surgical treatment which means you have management of pain relief, have an x-ray of the injury to confirm the dislocation and make sure that there is nothing broken. If it is a first time dislocation you will have rehabilitation through physio, strengthening the shoulder muscles and let the capsule repair itself. If it happens again then you would have to consider surgery. In this case you would have an operation where they tighten up the structure of either the front or the back of the shoulder, or they repair the 'cup' of the socket. There is a kind of cartilage called the labrum which they can tear off which makes the cup of the socket deeper. We would always go for surgical repair, as it is likely to happen again without it. The surgery is quite a painful procedure, but will see the player back in about four months. This would also take away the threat of it happening again, but what it could do is limit the range of movement, which has no effect on an outfield player. For a goalkeeper, you need to pick the right kind of surgery to make sure he maintains full movement.

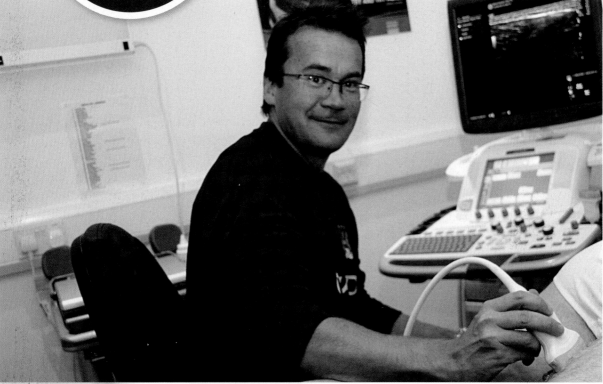

INVESTIGATION:

There are three grades of muscle tear: grade one, where there is swelling around the muscle fibres but they haven't been pulled apart. This takes seven to 10 days to recover from. Sometimes these can progress to the next grade though which is grade two, where the fibres have been pulled apart but they haven't completely ruptured. These are the most common hamstring tears and take anything from two to six weeks recovery time depending on the type of tear.

Grade three is when the fibres have been totally pulled apart and there's a rupture leaving a gap in the muscle. Upon examination, players with the grade three tear will sometimes have a hole in the muscle and the area fills up with blood.

DIAGNOSIS:

The best way to prevent a hamstring injury is not to get one in the first place! Hamstrings are muscles in the back of the leg above the knee and they control movement of both the knee and hip. They are an important structure for running so when a player pulls up with pain in the back of the thigh, we immediately fear a hamstring tear.

If this is the case, the player usually experiences pain at the back of the thigh and a feeling of weakness.

When we examine them, the first thing we do is feel along the muscle to see if there are any tender areas. We then move the leg to see if any certain movements cause pain along the hamstring area. We also do ultrasound scans which are used routinely on a daily basis to look at the muscles as this will show up if there is a tear. In some cases we use MRI scans to give us more detail.

TREATMENT:

The most severe tears need an operation to surgically put the muscle back together and require at least three months to recover from.

Hamstring tears can be prevented by a routine of good stretching, good warm-ups plus adequate preparation for training and the game. Prevention is the key as once you have had a hamstring injury there is a tendency for the injury to re-occur.

The management of the tear involves ice, compression and resting it to stop any further bleeding and to allow the muscle to heal. There are a number of other treatments that we use - we can inject the muscle with certain medications to speed up the healing process along with physiotherapy and rehabilitation programmes.

25

JOE HART GOALKEEPER

Born: 19/04/87 **Nationality:** English **Previous clubs:** Shrewsbury Town, Tranmere (loan), Blackpool (loan), Birmingham City (loan) **Career highlight:** Winning first England cap v Trinidad & Tobago in 2008 and winning Premier League Golden Gloves award for keeping 17 clean sheets during 2010/11.

30

COSTEL PANTILIMON GOALKEEPER

Born: 01/02/87 **Nationality:** Romanian
Previous clubs: Bacau, Timisoara II, Timisoara
Career highlight: Debut for Romania v Georgia in 2008.

12

STUART TAYLOR GOALKEEPER

Born: 28/11/80 **Nationality:** English
Previous clubs: Arsenal, Bristol Rovers (loan), Crystal Palace (loan), Peterborough (loan), Leicester (loan), Cardiff (loan), Aston Villa
Career highlight: Premier League winner's medal with Arsenal in 2001/02.

ALEKSANDAR KOLAROV
DEFENDER
13

Born: 10/11/85 **Nationality:** Serbian
Previous clubs: Lazio
Career highlight: Winning first cap for Serbia in 2008.

MICAH RICHARDS
DEFENDER
02

Born: 24/06/88 **Nationality:** English
Previous clubs: None
Career highlight: Scoring for England v Israel at Wembley in 2007.

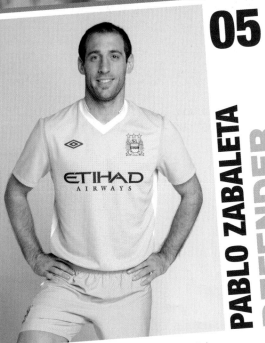

PABLO ZABALETA
DEFENDER
05

Born: 16/01/85 **Nationality:** Argentinian
Previous clubs: San Lorenzo, Espanyol
Career highlight: Winning gold medal for Argentina at 2008 Olympics.

38

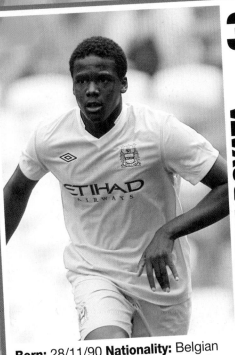

DEDRYCK BOYATA
DEFENDER

Born: 28/11/90 **Nationality:** Belgian
Previous clubs: Academy graduate
Career highlight: Making senior debut for City v Middlesbrough and winning first full cap for Belgium.

33

GREG CUNNINGHAM
DEFENDER

Born: 31/01/91 **Nationality:** Irish
Previous clubs: Leicester City (loan)
Career highlight: Making debut for Ireland v Paraguay in 2010.

15

STEFAN SAVIC
DEFENDER

Born: 08/01/91 **Nationality:** Montenegrin
Previous clubs: BSK Borca, Partizan Belgrade
Career highlight: Playing against England at Wembley in a 0-0 draw.

06

JOLEON LESCOTT
DEFENDER

Born: 16/08/82 **Nationality:** English
Previous clubs: Wolves, Everton
Career highlight: Making England debut v
Estonia 2007.

04

VINCENT KOMPANY
DEFENDER

Born: 10/04/86 **Nationality:** Belgian
Previous clubs: Anderlecht, Hamburg
Career highlight: International debut for Belgium
v France in 2004 aged 18, captaining City to FA
Cup semi-final win over Manchester United.

22

GAEL CLICHY
DEFENDER

Born: 25/07/85 **Nationality:** French
Previous clubs: Cannes, Arsenal
Career highlight: Part of the title-winning
'Invincibles' Arsenal side 0f 2003/04.

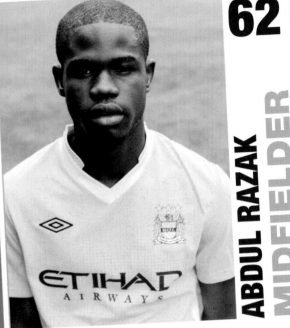

62

ABDUL RAZAK MIDFIELDER

Born: 11/11/92 **Nationality:** Ivorian
Previous clubs: None **Career highlight:**
Making senior debut v WBA in Feb 2011

28

KOLO TOURE DEFENDER

Born: 19/03/81 **Nationality:** Ivorian
Previous clubs: Arsenal
Career highlight: Representing Ivory Coast at
2010 World Cup.

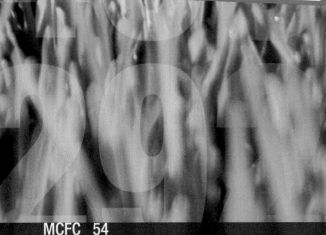

34

NIGEL DE JONG MIDFIELDER

Born: 30/11/84 **Nationality:** Dutch
Previous clubs: Ajax, Hamburg
Career highlight: Playing in 2010 World Cup
Final for Holland and scoring first City goal v
West Ham in April 2011.

08
SHAUN WRIGHT-PHILLIPS
MIDFIELDER

Born: 25/10/81 **Nationality:** English
Previous clubs: Chelsea **Career highlight:**
Scoring on his England debut v Ukraine 2004
and playing at 2010 World Cup.

07
JAMES MILNER
MIDFIELDER

Born: 04/01/86 **Nationality:** English
Previous clubs: Leeds United, Newcastle
United, Aston Villa **Career highlight:**
Representing England at 2010 World Cup.

18
GARETH BARRY
MIDFIELDER

Born: 23/02/81 **Nationality:** English
Previous clubs: Brighton, Aston Villa
Career highlight: First England cap v Ukraine
in 2002 and captaining England for the first
time v Egypt 2010.

MANCHESTER CITY FC
Squad Profiles 2012

11

ADAM JOHNSON
MIDFIELDER

Born: 14/07/87 **Nationality:** English
Previous clubs: Middlesbrough
Career highlight: Making England debut v Mexico in June 2010.

42

YAYA TOURE
MIDFIELDER

Born: 13/05/83 **Nationality:** Ivorian
Previous clubs: Beveren, Metalurh Donetsk, Olympiacos, Monaco, Barcelona
Career highlight: Winning 2009 UEFA Champions League with Barcelona and scoring winning goal in the 2011 FA Cup Final.

21

DAVID SILVA
MIDFIELDER

Born: 08/01/86 **Nationality:** Spanish
Previous clubs: Valencia, Eibar (loan), Celta Vigo (loan) **Career highlight:** Scoring two goals for Spain v Greece in August 2007.

16

SERGIO AGUERO STRIKER

Born: 02/06/88 **Nationality:** Argentinian
Previous clubs: Atletico Madrid
Career highlight: Voted La Liga 'Best Foreign Player' in 2008.

10

EDIN DZEKO STRIKER

Born: 17/03/86 **Nationality:** Bosnian
Previous clubs: FK Željezničar, FK Teplice, Wolfsburg **Career highlight:** First goal for Bosnia and being voted into the Wolfsburg Hall of Fame in 2011.

45

MARIO BALOTELLI STRIKER

Born: 12/08/90 **Nationality:** Italian
Previous clubs: Lumezzane, Inter Milan
Career highlight: Debut for Italy v Ivory Coast 2010 and winning 'Golden Boy Award' the same year – the top European honour for a player under 21.

Q&A
Joe Hart

What is the strangest thing you've been asked to sign?
"I remember once someone wanted me to sign someone's baby. I wasn't having any of that!"

Do you use oversized gloves or is it just an illusion?
"No, my gloves are actually really tight to be honest. I must have quite large hands then if people are thinking they're oversized."

Who do you think is the better player - Carlos Tevez now or Roberto Mancini when he was a player in Italy?
"I haven't seen Mancini when he was playing – but I'm going to have a guess and say that Carlos is better than the gaffer."

Who are your top 3 goalkeepers of all time?
"There are many goalkeepers that I admire but I think I can only say two that really stood out for me - David Seaman and Peter Schmeichel. They were top-class goalkeepers and legends of the game."

What would you like to do after retiring from football?

"I haven't actually thought about what I'm going to do afterwards. Right now I'm concentrating on my football and I'll see where it goes from there."

If you weren't a footballer what would you be?
"Football has always been what I wanted to do, if I hadn't got into football I honestly don't know what I would have done."

Do you see yourself staying at City for the rest of your career?
"If I was given the opportunity I would but at this moment I'm taking it season by season."

If you had to play in any other position on the pitch, where would it be?
"I'd be a striker - no doubt about that one."

Who do you class as your best mate at City and are you still mates with people at Birmingham?
"I've got loads of mates at City – but if I was going to pick anybody it would be Micah (Richards), I've known him the longest. I still get in

touch with the players, coaches and staff at Birmingham, they were great to me and I'm still mates with some of the players."

What does it take to be a top goalkeeper?
"The only advice I think I can give is work hard and just enjoy what you're doing - at any level of the game."

Goalkeepers are strange creatures, what is the strangest thing about you?
"I don't know if this is a strange thing – but I'm just ridiculously mad about football. It's always on my mind. When I go home I watch football, I'm just mad about it."

Would you ever be confident to step up and take a penalty?
"Yes!"

What's the strangest request that you've had from a fan?
"People seem to think that they can just ask you stupid questions and expect you to say yes to them, like for example someone said: 'Can I have your car?', that's the weirdest one I've been asked."

Spot the Ball

Use your instincts and the grid below to locate where you think the ball is located.

A   B   C   D   E   F

1
2
3
4
5
6
7
8

Answer on page 61

Quiz Answers

Spot the Difference #1 (From page 29)

Guess Who? #1 (From page 28)

ADAM JOHNSON

Guess Who? #2 (From page 34)

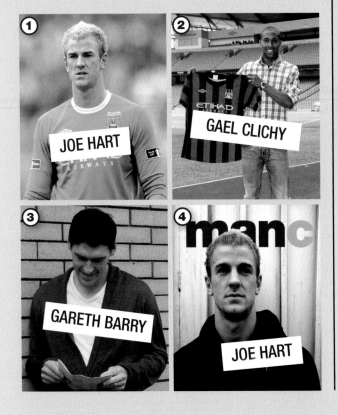

JOE HART

GAEL CLICHY

GARETH BARRY

JOE HART

Spot the Difference #2
(From page 45)

BIG CITY QUIZ - ANSWERS
(From page 30)

1. Lucky
2. Inter Milan
3. Edin Dzeko
4. Serbian
5. 29
6. Everton
7. Peter Crouch
8. 4
9. Dynamo Kyiv
10. True
11. 18
12. Nigel de Jong
13. Golden Boy Award
14. True
15. 4
16. Wolfsburg
17. True
18. Gran Canaria
19. 23
20. Take That

Spot the Ball
(From page 59)

Answer E4

WORDSEARCH #1 (From page 26)

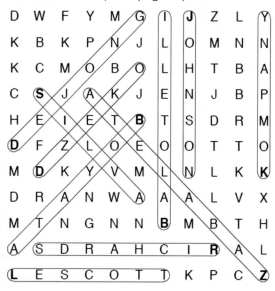

WORDSEARCH #2 (From page 44)

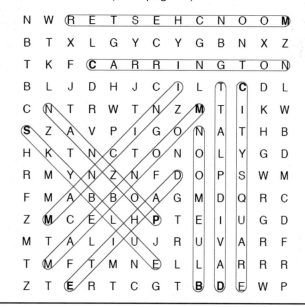

CROSSWORD SOLUTION (From page 35)

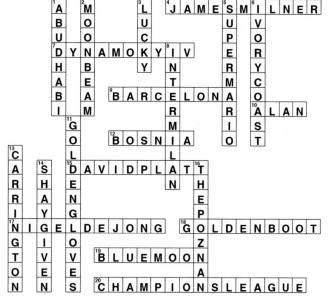

MCFC 61

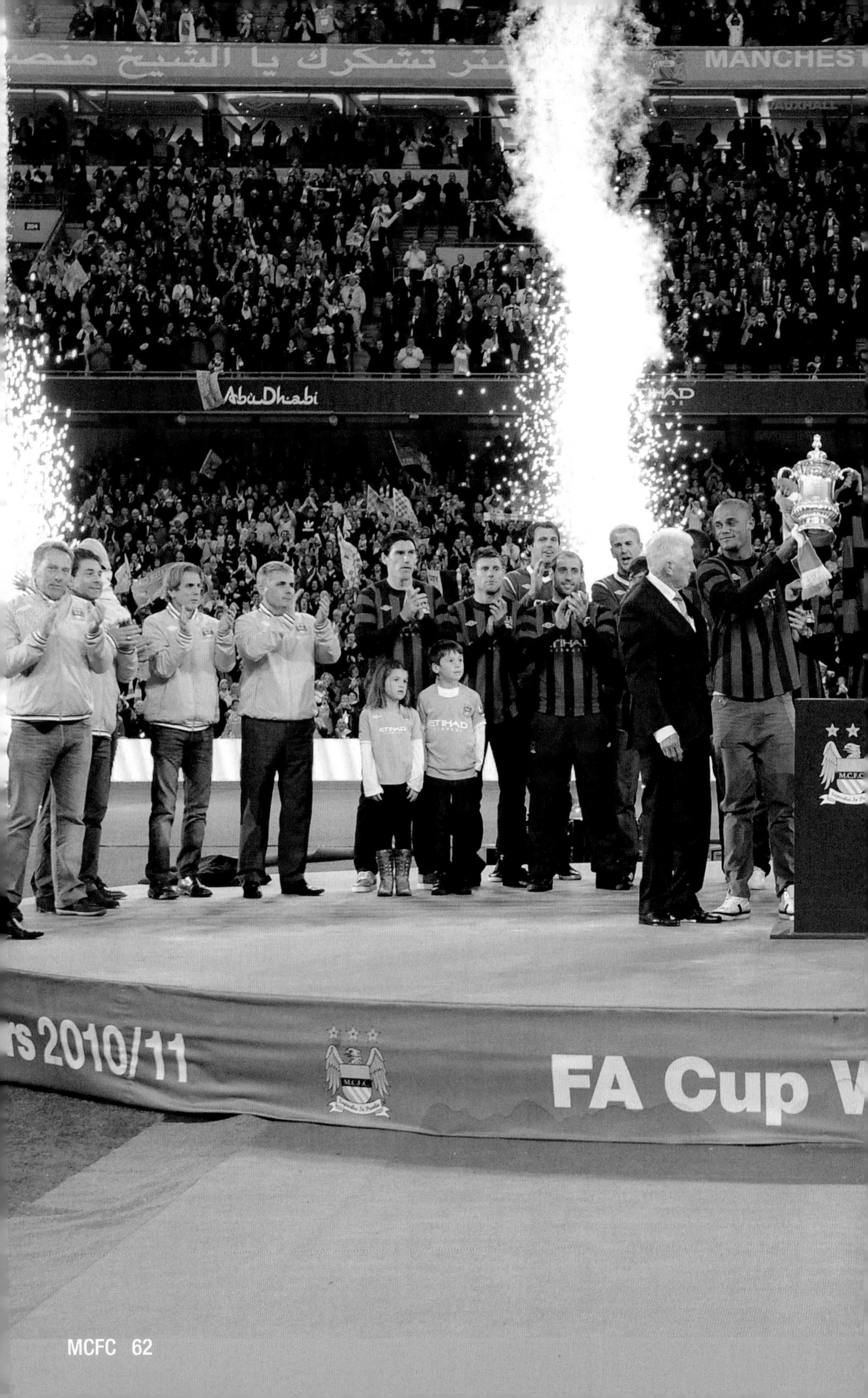
AbuDhabi
ETIHAD
rs 2010/11
FA Cup